CLINT EASTWOOD

66 *Quote Unquote* 99

CLINT EASTWOOD

"Quote Unquote"

Bob McCabe

CRESCENT
BOOKS

New York • Avenel

PICTURE ACKNOWLEDGEMENTS

Ronald Grant Archive: all pictures, including the front and back covers.

Every effort has been made to trace the copyright holders and we apologise in advance for any unintentional omissions. We would be pleased to insert the appropriate acknowledgement in any subsequent edition of this publication.

This 1996 edition is published by Crescent Books,
a division of Random House Value Publishing, Inc.,
40 Engelhard Avenue, Avenel, New Jersey 07001.

Crescent Books and colophon are registered trademarks of Random House Value Publishing, Inc.

Random House
New York ● Toronto ● London ● Sydney ● Auckland

First published in the UK in 1996

Copyright © Parragon Book Service Ltd 1996

ISBN: 0-517-18449-4

8 7 6 5 4 3 2 1

A CIP catalog record for this book is available from the Library of Congress

Produced by Haldane Mason, London

Editor: Paul Barnett
Design: Errol Campbell
Picture Research: Charles Dixon-Spain

Printed in Italy

CONTENTS

RAW TIMES TO RAWHIDE

'For years I bummed around trying to get a job and it was the same old story — my voice was too soft, my teeth needed capping, I squinted too much, I was too tall — all that constant tearing down of my ego was bound to turn me into a better person or a complete jerk. And I know that if I walked into a casting office right now and nobody knew I was Clint Eastwood, I'd get the same old thing. My voice is still too soft, my teeth still need capping, I still squint and I've been compared to a small redwood tree.'

The boy who would grow up to be the Man With No Name was in fact named for his father. Clinton Eastwood Jr entered the world on May 31 1930, born in St Francis Hospital in San Francisco as the son of 23-year-old salesman Clinton Senior (Sr) and 23-year-old housewife Ruth Eastwood. His father's family were Scots–English, his mother's Dutch–Irish – a good mix for a man who would later describe himself as the perfect Californian.

Clinton Sr was a stocks and bonds salesman who had the misfortune to find himself in the middle of the greatest depression his country had ever known. Work in general was scarce and in his field practically nonexistent, so the early years of Clint's life were spent travelling. 'It seems to me now that we didn't live much in houses at all: we lived in cars.'

A second child, Jean, was born during this itinerant period. The two children would often stay with their grandmother, who owned a chicken farm in Livermore.

'I didn't even get my own name.'

'I was about a foot taller than the rest of the kids. There were even occasions when I'd have lopped myself off at the knees if that had been possible.'

It was here that young Clint learned to ride. It was also here that his father taught him to fish, swim and shoot.

This constant moving around, coupled with his rapid growth – he was 6 ft 4 in tall by age 15 – left Clint with few close childhood friends.

It was around this time that life began to settle down in the Eastwood household. Clinton Sr landed a permanent job with the Container Corporation of America, and the family returned to settle in Oakland, where Clint enrolled at Oakland Technical High. An English teacher there, Miss Jones, played an instrumental part – albeit unknowingly – in shaping Clint's life. Impressed by his stature she insisted he took the lead in a school play. 'The prospect terrified me,' he later recalled. 'I didn't think it was possible to act, even in a school play, unless you were an extrovert.'

RIGHT: An early studio publicity shot.

'It was just one of those things: we instantly identified with each other. We weren't that excited about going to school; both being sort of non-joiners, non-members of the pack. Clint had tremendous athletic ability all through high school but, not being a keen-spirited-type guy, never really followed it through.'

FRITZ MANES

RIGHT: The character of Rowdy Yates was to lead Clint into some of the most lucrative and critically acclaimed Western roles Hollywood has ever produced.

It was also at Oakland Tech that Eastwood met his life-long friend Fritz Manes, who would later become an executive at his production company and produce several of his movies. The two, both of them outsiders, became best buddies.

Clint's early life travelling and the time spent on his grandmother's farm had given him a taste for the outdoor life. Inspired by the tough times he'd seen his family go through, Clint spent the summer of his 16th year earning

RIGHT: *The sound of Charlie 'Bird' Parker began Eastwood's lifelong love of jazz.*

money by baling hay, working to the point of exhaustion but once again enjoying the outdoor lifestyle. 'That was about the happiest time of my life till then.'

With two friends – Bob Sturges and Jack McKnight – Clint also indulged a new-found passion for drag racing, and when the summer came along the three of them headed off to work in the Lassen Volcanic National Park. The work was arduous – clearing stretches of undergrowth to prevent fire spreading from Mount Lassen, one of the few active volcanoes in the United States – but Eastwood was in his element.

In 1945 Clint heard a young alto-sax player named Charlie 'Bird' Parker, and so began a life-long passion for jazz. Over 40 years later, he would direct and produce the tragic and brief biography of the Bird on film; now it inspired him to learn trumpet and piano. He studied hard, and within two years landed a job playing piano at the Omar Club in Oakland.

He also found work at a pulp mill in Springfield, Oregon. It was here, largely as a result of his search for available girls, that he discovered country and western, another musical form that would later play a significant part in his work, from

'Somebody told me to go to this place where there was a lot of country music. I wasn't very interested but this guy told me there were a lot of girls there. So I went. I saw Bob Wills and his Texas Playboys. Unlike most country bands, they had brass and reeds and they played country swing. They were good. It surprised me a little bit how good they were. Also, there were a lot of girls there, which didn't surprise me at all. So I guess you could say that lust expanded my musical horizons.'

ON DISCOVERING COUNTRY & WESTERN

---

the soundtrack of movies such as *Every Which Way but Loose* to the lead character and background of *Honkytonk Man*.

At the age of 40 Clinton Sr secured the job with the Georgia-Pacific Timber Company that would eventually make him a wealthy man. The job meant relocating his family to Seattle, and young Clint wasted no time in taking full advantage of the terrain, trying his hand at lumberjacking here in the great Pacific North West. In fact, during this period he did a number of jobs: swimming instructor, lifeguard, steel worker and truck driver. Realizing he was drifting, Clint decided to give college a try, majoring in music.

But the Korean War put a halt to his plans. He was drafted and shipped out for basic training at Fort Ord, on the coast of Monterey. As luck would have it, while his comrades in arms were being sent overseas, Eastwood became the camp's swimming instructor. It was a cushy number, but it was not enough to retain his interest and so, against army regulations, he took a variety of civilian jobs off-base, including work as a bouncer at the officers' club and as a relief cinema projectionist. Only once while he was in the army did he see anything like action. He hitched a ride to San Francisco aboard a navy bomber whose engine cut out about 2 km (1 mile) from shore, so the pilot was forced to land the plane in water. It was an unexpectedly dramatic end to Clint's army days.

Two significant events occurred in his life during this period. First, on his weekends away from camp he discovered the seaside town of Carmel, a place he would later call home and of which he would one day become mayor. Second, shortly after his discharge, he met Maggie Johnson.

In May 1953 Maggie was a student at the University of California at Berkeley. Two months after their first meeting, she graduated, and headed back to her parents in Los Angeles. Eastwood followed her and, once there, enrolled in a business administration course at the Los Angeles City College. As was by now typical of him, he found a number of jobs to boost his income – he halved his rent by becoming the janitor for the apartment building where he lived, and he pumped gas, delivered cars and worked as a lifeguard at weekends.

On December 19 1953, following a seven-month courtship, Clint Eastwood and Maggie Johnson were married. They honeymooned in Carmel. With marriage the time had come for him to give up his series of casual jobs and settle down to a career. His business course wasn't really showing him the way forward, so he parlayed a chance meeting into a screen test. At Fort Ord he had met director Arthur Lubin, who was filming for a few days on location at the fort. Impressed by the sol-dier's looks, Lubin told Clint to contact him at Universal Studios. This Clint now did, and, two weeks after his screen test, he was offered a six-month contract at $75 a week.

Although on-screen work was long in coming, during those first six months Eastwood took full advantage of Universal's acting classes, slowly learning the rudiments of his new profession; he

'I don't like the idea of getting killed, of anybody getting killed, but especially me. I'm against war, all war, and when I was in the army, I was against the Korean War.'

supplemented these by taking additional acting classes in the evening, at his own expense. He took them 'with my eyes open and my big mouth shut' and, remarkably, continued to attend them for the next 15 years. All he needed now was a little help from the Creature from the Black Lagoon.

In 1955, Clint Eastwood made his somewhat ignominious cinematic debut in *The Revenge of the Creature* as lab assistant

RIGHT: *The 'very attractive' Clint Eastwood assists Ginger Rodgers as* The First Travelling Saleslady *(1956).*

Jennings, his one line being: 'I've lost my white mouse.' Then *Creature* director Jack Arnold hired Eastwood for another small role, in Arnold's next science-fiction movie, *Tarantula* (1955). In this classic B-movie tale of a giant rampaging spider,

Eastwood hid behind goggles as the pilot who dropped the big one on the eight-legged marauder.

This was as good as it got for the young actor over the next few years: he was just another bit-part player who

BELOW: Ambush at
Cimarron Pass (1958)
– 'Probably the worst
movie ever made.'

appeared in a string of forgettable movies. Arthur Lubin helped his protégé out with similar small roles in some of his productions – least notably in *Lady Godiva* (1955), in which Clint, playing the role of 'First Saxon', was listed at the very bottom of the credits. Another Lubin casting of Clint was opposite Francis the talking mule in *Francis in the Navy* (1955).

As bad as the roles were, Eastwood was determined to exploit the experience, spending as much time as he could hanging out on set, talking to the technicians, gradually learning the process of making movies.

In 1956, he made his first appearance in a Western – an unaccredited role in *Star in the Dust* – turned in a similarly low-key appearance opposite Rock Hudson in *Never Say Goodbye*, and found

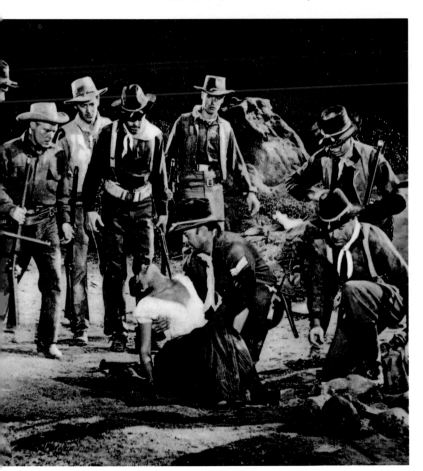

BELOW: Ambush at Cimarron Pass (1958) – 'Probably the worst movie ever made.'

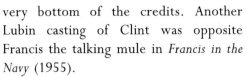

'I finally got to a state where I was really depressed. The movie finally came out and I went with my wife down to a little neighbourhood theatre and it was so bad I said to Maggie, 'I'm going to quit, I'm really going to quit. I've got to start doing something with my life.'
ON AMBUSH AT CIMARRON PASS

his contract with Universal at an end. 'After a year and a half, they booted me out, along with a lot of other contract players.'

Once again Arthur Lubin came through, this time securing Clint a contract with RKO Radio Pictures, and a chance at a decent role. Eastwood played Carol Channing's romantic interest in the comedy Western *The First Travelling Saleslady* (1956). It was by no means a star-making role, but it did garner the young actor his first review in the *Hollywood Reporter*, which labelled him 'very attractive'.

Roles in Lubin's *Escapade in Japan* (1957) and *Lafayette Escardille* (UK title *Hell Bent for Glory*) followed, but Eastwood nevertheless found himself forced to take on extra labouring work, digging swimming pools for his would-be colleagues in Beverly Hills. *Ambush at Cimarron Pass* (1958) offered Eastwood third billing, his most prestigious credit to date. 'It was probably the worst movie ever made,' he has said, not inaccurately. When it was released, Eastwood underwent a crisis of confidence, wondering whether he had done the right thing in choosing a career in acting, and he briefly considered giving up the profession.

LEFT: Two chaps with chaps — Rowdy Yates (Eastwood) with trail-boss Gil Favor (Eric Fleming) in Rawhide.

'TV was like a younger brother, or a second-class citizen, but to me it was a logical place to really learn the business.'

In between movie appearances, Eastwood had begun to work on numerous television shows – *Highway Patrol*, *Navy Log* and *Man of Annapolis* among them. He even landed a semi-regular role as a rookie cadet in 12 episodes of *West Point*. When he heard that CBS was looking for someone to play the second lead in their new Western series, *Rawhide*, he managed – through the help of Sonia Chernus, an old friend of Maggie's who was now working at the network – to get a test for the role of Rowdy Yates. Handed a lengthy page of emotive dialogue, he decided to improvise around the text. The director was not too happy, but the studio executives thought Clint really looked the part, and so he got it. Sent on location to Arizona, Eastwood carefully studied the techniques he was shown for working the herd, eager to ensure he looked as close to the real thing as possible.

RIGHT: Rowdy Yates plays away from home. The Spanish Countess (Linda Cristal) is saved from murderous Comancheros by our hero in the Rawhide *episode called 'Incident of the Burst of Evil'.*

RIGHT: Rawhide *made Clint Eastwood a pin-up.*

PHOTOPLAY

CLINT EASTWOOD
"RAWHIDE"

'I tell people, if you really want to do it, then you must be willing to study it and stick with it through all opposition and having to deal with some of the most no-talent people in the world passing judgement on you. If you can take all that and keep grinding until some part comes along that fits you and your feelings, then sometimes the odds will come up for you. People think I play "anger" well; all you have to do is have a good memory.'
ON HIS PRE-RAWHIDE DAYS IN HOLLYWOOD

Then, with 10 episodes already filmed, CBS abruptly cancelled *Rawhide*. By Christmas 1958 Clint was once again giving serious consideration to abandoning acting altogether when a telegram arrived telling him that *Rawhide* had, after all, been picked up by the network and would air in the New Year. He was to get himself back out on location immediately.

The first episode of *Rawhide*, accompanied by Frankie Laine's distinctive theme song, aired on Friday January 9 1959. It went on to become a huge hit, running for a total of 217 episodes over seven seasons. Bit-part movie actor Clint Eastwood was now a major TV star.

While working on *Rawhide*, Eastwood was devoting most of his spare time to studying all aspects of moviemaking. 'We did 200 hours of that show. I think I learned more from that than almost anything I've ever done.' Other distractions for the star were of a more human nature. Shooting on location meant long periods away from Maggie, and it was clear from the start that Eastwood did not intend to remain faithful to her. On the set of *Rawhide* he met actress Roxanne Tunis. They began an affair and on June 17 1964 Roxanne gave birth to the actor's first child, daughter Kimber. Eastwood acknowledged his responsibilities, paying for the upkeep of the child in exchange for Roxanne's silence. All parties adhered to this deal for 25 years.

The producers of the show agreed to let Clint direct an episode. Unfortunately the network, having already experienced difficulties with actors on other shows taking control behind the camera, vetoed the plan, putting the Eastwood directing debut on hold.

It was not just the lack of directing opportunities that were now turning Eastwood against *Rawhide*. The long shooting schedule and a restrictive contract were forcing him to turn down big-screen offers. The only opportunity he'd had to appear elsewhere was playing himself opposite a talking horse in the television series *Mr Ed*. *Clint Eastwood Meets Mr Ed* was directed by the actor's early patron, Arthur Lubin. It probably represents Eastwood's least-seen screen appearance.

Then, in 1964, he got a chance to get back on the big screen, although initially the offer to star in an Italian Western being shot in Spain did not seem to resemble a passport to movie stardom.

Novice Italian director Sergio Leone, inspired by the huge success of *The Magnificent Seven* (1960) – itself a Western remake of Akira Kurosawa's *Seven Samurai* (1954) – planned to adapt another of Kurosawa's classics, *Yojimbo* (1961), as a Western. Eager to exploit the connection, the movie was to be called *The Magnificent Stranger*. Charles Bronson, Henry Fonda and James Coburn had all declined the lead role. Leone had no idea who Clint Eastwood was until he chanced upon an episode of *Rawhide*

LEFT: Eastwood in colour, on a fence, in Rawhide contemplating those ever-present cattle.

'I wanted to direct, way back when I was doing Rawhide. *I'd been assigned to direct an episode, but the network reneged. So I directed some trailers and various coming-attraction things for the next season of the series, then I let it lie.'*

entitled 'Incident of the Black Sheep'. He was impressed, and the actor's price was right (Eastwood in fact received $15,000 for his first starring role). But he was intrigued by Leone's offer and, after consulting with Maggie, decided to take a gamble on this Italian-German-Spanish co-production. 'If the picture turns out to be a bomb, it won't go anywhere,' Eastwood reasoned to his agent.

Clint arrived on location in Almeria in May 1964 for what turned out to be an extremely fraught shoot. Speaking no Spanish or Italian, and with no one else speaking anything more than rudimentary English, he found himself isolated from the cast and crew. All the cast spoke their lines in their various native tongues, since Leone planned to dub everything later. Consequently no one bar Leone himself knew what was going on most of the time.

Ironically, these communication difficulties worked in Eastwood's favour when he decided to pare down Leone's dialogue to its bare minimum. This approach secured the character who came to be known as the Man With No Name, and would directly establish Eastwood's minimalist screen persona.

Pour une Poignée de Dollars

FACING PAGE: A poncho, a cheroot and a hat full of attitude – The Magnificent Stranger rides into town.

Another significant element in the success of what was soon labelled a 'Spaghetti Western' was the unconventional music score, composed by Leone's childhood friend Ennio Morricone.

Eastwood provided his own costume for the movie, borrowing the gunbelt from the prop box of *Rawhide*, but this

was only one example of how the production was walking a financial tightrope. One day, after the crew had not been paid for two weeks, Eastwood arrived on set to find it totally deserted. 'I've always been a loner but suddenly I was literally the most alone man in all Spain,' he later joked.

Although Eastwood enjoyed playing the Western anti-hero, he had no big hopes for *The Magnificent Stranger* when he flew back to the United States to begin the seventh season of *Rawhide*. Then one day on set, reading *Variety*, he came across a piece about the coming vogue of Italian Westerns, following the success of *A Fistful of Dollars*. He thought nothing more of it until two days later when he learned that *A Fistful of Dollars* was the new title for *The Magnificent Stranger* and it was going through the roof.

At least in Europe, Clint Eastwood was now what he had long wanted to be – a *bona fide* movie star.

> '*The story is told that, when Michelangelo was asked what he had seen in one particular block of marble, which he chose among hundreds of others, he replied that he saw Moses. I would offer the same answer to the question why did I choose Clint Eastwood, only backwards. When they ask me what I saw in Clint Eastwood, who was playing I don't know what kind of second-rate role in a Western television series in 1964, I reply that what I saw, simply, was a block of marble.*'
> SERGIO LEONE

COUNTING THE DOLLARS

'I think they changed the approach to Westerns.
They "operacized" them, if there's such a word.
They made the violence and the shooting aspect
a little larger than life, and they had great
music and new types of scores.'

By 1965 Eastwood was a huge star in Europe – particularly in Italy, where his cheroot-chomping anti-hero was known simply as 'Il Cigarillo'. When Sergio Leone offered him $50,000, a percentage of the profits and a brand new Ferrari, he was only too pleased to don poncho once more and head back to Spain to film a sequel, initially titled (in all seriousness) *Two Magnificent Strangers*. Once again Charles Bronson passed up the opportunity to work with Leone, declining the role of the second stranger; the part eventually went to Lee Van Cleef.

An increased budget ensured that on *For a Few Dollars More* (1965) – as the movie became – there were none of the production problems that had plagued the first movie, allowing Leone to develop his distinctive 'pop' Western visuals, blending vast vistas with stark sun-worn close-ups, all set to Ennio Morricone's witty, pulsating score.

While Clint was dubbing the movie in Italy, legendary Italian director Vittorio de Sica persuaded him to make a cameo appearance in his segment of an anthology movie, *The Witches* (1966).

Before heading back to 'move 'em on, head 'em up' once more in *Rawhide*, Eastwood inked a deal with Leone for a third Spaghetti Western, to be made the following year. He secured himself a quarter of a million dollars, plus ten percent of the box office in the Western Hemisphere.

Eastwood was eager to recreate his movie success Stateside and also by now bored with his yearly commitment to *Rawhide*, so it was fortunate for him when the show was cancelled, on February 8 1966. In addition to the freedom he needed to pursue his movie career, he received from CBS a pay-off cheque for $119,000.

Showing a distinct lack of imagination, Sergio Leone initially called his third Spaghetti Western *The Magnificent Rogues*.

'I'm probably the highest-paid American actor who ever worked in Italian pictures. Only Mastroianni gets more in Italy. For the first time in my life, I can pick the parts I want to play.'

ON FINDING FINANCIAL SUCCESS IN EUROPE

"FOR A FEW DOLLARS MORE"(X)
starring **CLINT EASTWOOD**
also starring **LEE VAN CLEEF**
GIAN MARIA VOLONTE
Directed by **SERGIO LEONE**
Produced by Alberto Grimaldi
Print by Technicolor   Released through United Artists

LEFT: Lee Van Cleef and Clint Eastwood — Two Magnificent Strangers!

ABOVE: Clint Eastwood in the Italian drama The Witches, *with Silvana Mangano.*

'Rawhide *was great fun at first and it was certainly a great training-ground. But after seven years of playing the same character in the same wardrobe you get kind of edgy and the wardrobe begins to stand up all by itself. After a while, you have to think of things to keep yourself amused. And when you find yourself putting lipgloss on your horse you know you're becoming ill.'*

Making a hat-trick of lost opportunity, Charles Bronson turned down a role in the movie once again, leaving Eli Wallach and Lee Van Cleef, returning in a different role, as Eastwood's co-stars. By far the most ambitious of Leone's trilogy, *The Good, The Bad and The Ugly* (1966) – as it was retitled – was a sprawling three-hour style-epic, with a higher emphasis on humour than before and with Morricone's best – and most imitated – score to date: Eastwood himself years later parodied the famous whistled theme in a fight scene in *Every Which Way but Loose* (1978). Curiously, if we take it that Eastwood's stranger is the same character in the trilogy, then this movie acts as a prequel to the others, set as it is during the Civil War, whereas the earlier movies are set after that war.

The Good, The Bad and The Ugly was a box-office success throughout Europe and Japan, and finally the three films were sold, as one package, to the United States

in 1967. Although generally referred to now as the Man With No Name, Eastwood's stranger is in fact briefly referred to as 'Joe' in the first movie and 'Blondie' in the third. The monicker of 'the Man With No Name' was devised for the US poster campaign when the movies were released in the United States.

A Fistful of Dollars opened on 80 screens in New York on February 2 1967, and was rewarded by huge returns; *For A few Dollars More* repeated this success in May; *The Good, The Bad and The Ugly* did likewise when it was released the following year.

Finally, Eastwood was a star in his own land.

The success of the *Dollars* trilogy in the United States confirmed what

RIGHT: For A Few Dollars More *original Spanish poster art.*

'In the beginning, I was just about alone. Then there were two. And now there are three of us. I'm going to end up in a detachment of cavalry.'
ON THE GOOD, THE BAD AND THE UGLY

RIGHT: The man who put spaghetti into the Western – Sergio Leone.

'*Of all the actors of the new generation, it is Clint Eastwood who gives me the most hope. He is the best cowboy of modern cinema.*'
JOHN WAYNE

Eastwood had felt about the series from the beginning – the US Western had grown stale and uninventive, thanks to the fact that stars like John Wayne had been playing the same kind of role in the same kind of movie for decades. Eastwood was a youthful Western star and, more importantly, in the age of Vietnam and social unrest in the United States, he was clearly an anti-hero, not advocating the good guy over the bad guy but subtly blurring the edges between the two. As *New Yorker* critic Pauline Kael succinctly noted in her unfavourable review of the *Dollars* movies, 'This is no longer the romantic world where the hero is, fortunately, the best shot; instead, the best shot is the hero.'

Having finally achieved the status he desired, Eastwood wasted no time in exploiting it. His first move was to set up his own production company, something that is standard for almost any actor in Hollywood these days but which in 1967 was practically unheard-of. His handling of Malpaso Productions (Malpaso being Spanish for 'bad step') proved that, although he never finished his business degree in college, he put what he had learned to good use. Housed at Universal Studios, Malpaso essentially existed to hire out independently the services of its main asset, Clint Eastwood, so allowing him to maintain as much control as possible over all his projects.

RIGHT: Coogan calls the bad guy's bluff in the frontier town of New York.

Hang 'Em High (1967) was the first Malpaso production, and it owed more than a passing resemblance to the Leone films. Directed by Ted Post, with whom Eastwood had worked on *Rawhide*, this tale of a man wreaking revenge on the gang who strung him up and left him for dead was basically the Man With No Name relocated Stateside. But, if Eastwood's philosophy was if it ain't broke, don't fix it, he was proved right at the box office when *Hang 'Em High* went into profit faster than any other movie in United Artists' history, making its budget back in just its first weekend, eventually outgrossing all of the *Dollars* films in the States. Flexing his business acumen, Eastwood picked up $400,000 for his performance, plus 25 percent of the gross – all in all, a highly lucrative deal for a low-budget movie!

In learning his craft as a director, Eastwood always cites three main influences – Leone, Ted Post and Don Siegel. Siegel was the man hired to be the director of Eastwood's next vehicle, the cop thriller *Coogan's Bluff* (1968).

Eastwood's first few years working back in the United States were largely an experimental period for him, in which, while always keeping one eye on the box

'Hollywood was suspicious for a long time. So few actors had come out of television series to go into cinema, they were very, very suspicious. It wasn't until all three of those Leone films that I did one or two American films.'

office, he geared himself up for directing while at the same time taking on a variety of projects designed to help expand his range and his on-screen persona.

Coogan's Bluff was the first of these projects. Eastwood played Walt Coogan, an Arizona sheriff sent to Manhattan to extradite a prisoner. Essentially, the dress and the image were still that of the lone Western hero, but transposed to a modern setting, cleverly diversifying Eastwood's image without straying too far from what he knew his audience

> *'I like those characters myself, that's why I carry them to other extremes than my predecessors. In other words, in the complications of society as we know it today, sometimes a person who can cut through the bureaucracy and red tape is a hero. A person who can do that, a man who thinks on a very simple level and has very simple moral values, appeals to a great many people.'*

> *'The films that I did with Sergio, if they'd been done with less style, they would have been very poor shows because they weren't really good strong stories, and I like stories. It's not that we drifted apart, but I think we just became philosophically different.'*

expected. Ironically, while developing this cowboy image, he created the prototype for what would become his most durable creation, Dirty Harry. With the character of Coogan, Eastwood first essayed the maverick cop forced to battle authority and bureaucracy as much as crime, in essence the screen's late-20th-century equivalent of the cowboy and the beginnings of Harry Callahan.

With *Coogan's Bluff*, Eastwood found the theme of character he had been searching for, a means of bringing the values of the Western into the present day. Also, he had the opportunity to learn a great deal by working with Siegel, who included a brief nod to Eastwood's undistinguished early days in the movies (as Coogan walks through a hippie-infested nightclub, a scene from *Tarantula* is briefly projected behind him). The movie was once again a box-office winner, and also provided the inspiration for the long-running 1970s TV series *McCloud*, starring Dennis Weaver.

Furthermore, it provided Eastwood with some sort of blueprint for the future, although he still had some experimenting to do before he could build on it.

Eastwood's decision to star in *Where Eagles Dare* (1969), based on the Alistair MacLean novel, was twofold. First, it

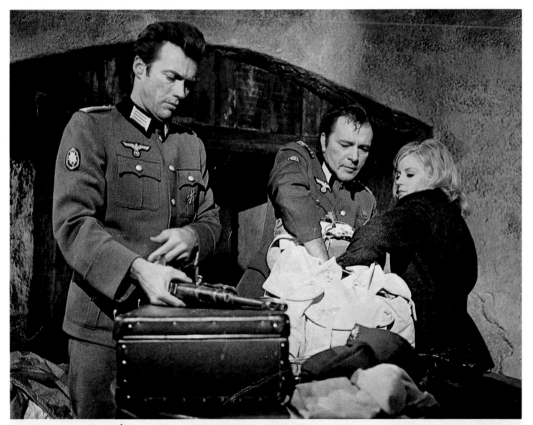

METRO-GOLDWYN-MAYER presents RICHARD BURTON · CLINT EASTWOOD in "WHERE EAGLES DARE" A

LEFT: Burton speaks! Eastwood shoots! Where Eagles Dare *(1969)*

ABOVE: Smile if you enjoyed Paint Your Wagon! *(1969).*

himself presented on-screen, once again paring away large passages of dialogue – as he had done with Leone's first screen-play.

Four days before *Where Eagles Dare* wrapped in May 1968, Maggie gave birth to a son, Kyle Clinton. Eastwood celebrated with the Burtons and flew home as soon as he could to be with his family. But, despite the presence of this new son at home, he was quick to pack up for another movie involving a protracted location shoot. During his *Rawhide* days, Eastwood had briefly tried his hand at singing, releasing a single, 'Unknown Girl' on Gothic Records. *Paint Your Wagon* (1969) gave him another chance to test out his vocals – now in a screen allowed him to try his hand at a new genre – the war movie and second, as a large-scale all-star production, it offered him a chance to hold his own on screen against other big names, including in this case Richard Burton.

Having finished shooting on *Coogan's Bluff* on December 31 1967, Clint celebrated the New Year by flying to Austria to begin *Where Eagles Dare* on January 2. He was adamant about how he wanted

'It was instructive to watch Clint move around because he reduced everything to an absolute minimum. If he had a four-line speech, he would reduce it to four words and it was enormously effective.'
RICHARD BURTON

'We decided to let Richard's character handle the exposition — he has a beautiful speaking voice and he's very good at that sort of thing — and I would handle the shooting which they felt I was very good at.'
ON WHERE EAGLES DARE

As soon as I light the powd you drive the arrow through and pull it out

UNIVERSAL PRESENTS **CLINT EASTWOOD** in A MARTIN RACKIN PRODUCTION "TWO MULES FOR TECHNIC **SHIRLEY MACLAINE** SISTER SARA" A PANAVIS

version of a Lerner-Loewe musical, with a screenplay by Paddy Chayevsky. As with *Eagles*, Clint took second billing, this time to Lee Marvin.

The movie was shot in Baker, Oregon, and proved something of a profligate disaster. As a moviemaker, Eastwood has always believed strongly in being cost-effective, and likely a lot of that feeling stemmed from his experience on *Paint Your Wagon*. 'It was a disaster, but it didn't have to be such an expensive disaster,' he said. 'We had Lear jets flying everyone in and out of Oregon, helicopters to take the wives to location for lunch, crews of seven trucks, thousands of extras getting paid for doing nothing, everyone living in ranch houses

— 20 million dollars down the drain and most of it doesn't even show on the screen.'

Paint Your Wagon failed to set the box office on fire, but Eastwood walked away from it with a lesson on how not to make movies, and $750,000 richer.

Sensing that he was beginning to stray too far from what audiences identified him with, he decided to make his next project a Western . . . of sorts. Still

ABOVE: Shirley MacLaine draws blood — Two Mules For Sister Sara (1969).

intrigued by the dynamic of acting against other stars and wishing to bring more humour into his Man With No Name persona, Eastwood opted to go with a project to which Elizabeth Taylor had introduced him on the set of *Where Eagles Dare*. *Two Mules for Sister Sara* (1969) was a comedy Western; the plot involves a lone drifter (Eastwood) becoming embroiled with a nun (Shirley MacLaine), who turns out to be a prostitute.

Eastwood brought Don Siegel on board as director. But, as with *Paint Your Wagon*, it was a role that demanded he play second fiddle to the other lead, not a role for which he was either cut out or comfortable with. Add to this a genuine antipathy between Eastwood and co-star MacLaine, and *Two Mules for Sister Sara* became a dreary experience, redeemed only by Siegel's impressive handling of the action scenes and for the fact that it helped to bond the growing friendship between director and star.

Despite the ups and downs of this period, Eastwood's movies were still delivering at the box office, and it was partly this that kept him experimenting on screen. The other factor was that deep down he knew he still hadn't found a screen persona that equalled the one he had had in his break-through *Dollars* movies.

Kelly's Heroes (1970) re-teamed the actor with *Where Eagles Dare* director Brian G. Hutton. It was a strong anti-war comedy set in World War II, but presenting a perfect satiric message in light of the ongoing anti-Vietnam feeling in the United States. Eastwood headlined an all-star cast that included Donald Sutherland, Telly Savalas and comedian Don Rickles, the man who memorably characterized Clint as 'the only man who can talk with flies on his lips'.

In 1968 Clint Eastwood was the number-five box office attraction in the United States; by 1970 he had risen to number two, and his lifestyle was beginning to reflect this success. *Rawhide* had bought the Eastwoods their first house, in Sherman Oaks. Movie money had allowed them to add on a pool, a gym and a games room. The *Dollars* movies allowed them to buy property in Clint's dream town of Carmel. By 1969, they had rebuilt their small vacation house, complete with their own private beach.

Maggie had grown to accept Clint behaving as what he termed a 'married bachelor', and their life together, whenever he wasn't working, was dominated

RIGHT: 'The only man who can talk with flies on his lips' – Kelly's Heroes *(1970).*

M-G-M presents "KELLY'S HEROES", Panavision ® Metrocolor ®

by their interest in sport – golf for him, tennis for her – and Eastwood's predilection for healthy living. He was working out, drinking herbal tea and extolling the wonders of vitamins years before these became compulsory in Hollywood.

In 1971, Eastwood brought Don Siegel in to direct the relatively low-key *The Beguiled*, in which Clint himself played a wounded Yankee soldier forced to take refuge in a girls' school while hiding from the Confederates.

The Beguiled was Eastwood's least-profitable film to date, earning mixed reviews in the United States but, continuing a trend that would remain throughout Eastwood's career, it was both a critical and a box-office smash in Europe, finding particular favour with the French critics.

Eastwood was slowly assembling on these early Malpaso productions a team behind the camera of whom many would remain with him for years. Cinematographer Bruce Surtees became an integral part of the team following his work on *The Beguiled*, as did musician Lalo Schifrin, with whom Eastwood had first worked on *Kelly's Heroes*.

Despite the financial disappointment of *The Beguiled*, Eastwood felt he was finally ready to turn his hand to directing. *Play Misty for Me* (1970) was another uncharacteristic piece – he played a radio DJ pursued by a psychotic female listener – but he promised the studio he'd make it for less than $1 million, waiving his usual fee in favour of a percentage of the film's profits.

Eastwood turned the tables by persuading Don Siegel to act in the movie, as a bartender. 'I knew I'd have a really good director on the set if anything went wrong,' he joked at the time.

BELOW: Sufferin' in the South – The Beguiled *(1970).*

'*Clint Eastwood is a man who knows where he's going. In an age of uncertainty in the arts, politics and everything else, people enjoy watching a man like this in action.*'
BRIAN G. HUTTON

Universal Presents A MALPASO COMPANY PRODUCTION
CLINT EASTWOOD
in **PLAY MISTY FOR ME** x
JESSICA   DONNA   JOHN
WALTER   MILLS   LARCH

*ABOVE: Fan adulation —
Play Misty For Me
(1970)*

'One of the reasons I wanted to make The Beguiled is that it is a woman's picture, not a picture for women, but about them. Women are capable of deceit, larceny, murder, anything. Behind that mask of innocence lies just as much evil as you'll find in members of the Mafia.'
DON SIEGEL

Establishing what would quickly become a pattern in his movies, Eastwood brought in *Play Misty for Me* four days ahead of schedule and $50,000 under budget. 'In the past accolades have been bestowed unfairly, primarily on the motion-picture directors who have spent most time and money on their pictures.' Establishing another work pattern as a director, Eastwood spent his evenings editing the movie while still shooting, converting a room above his Carmel restaurant, the Hog's Breath Inn, for this purpose.

Much to the surprise of the studio and its director, *Play Misty For Me* easily recouped its investment at the box office, Eastwood's percentage working out just fine, as audiences responded to this proto-*Fatal Attraction*. The film was also well received critically: Clint Eastwood finally convinced Hollywood and himself that he was a director to be reckoned with.

FINDING THE PERFECT ANTI-HERO

'I know what you're thinking, punk. Did he fire six shots or only five? To tell you the truth, in all the excitement, I kind of lost track myself. But being that this is a .44 magnum, the most powerful hand gun in the world and would blow your head clean off, you got to ask yourself one question, "Do I feel lucky?" Well, do you, punk?'

AS DIRTY HARRY

FACING PAGE: *Re-painting the Western in Hellish hues* – High Plains Drifter *(1972).*

In July 1971 Clint Eastwood featured on the cover of *Life* under the somewhat unflattering headline 'The world's favourite movie star is – no kidding – Clint Eastwood'. A Golden Globe award that year and a bronze medallion for his artistic contribution to the Italian film industry only added to Eastwood's status as the world's biggest box-office star.

Ironically, this success had been achieved on the back of a number of diverse movies, several of which did not show their star off to best effect. His career might have made him number one at the box office, but Eastwood knew that, if he were to maintain that position, he had to find the ingredient that his first eight US films had lacked. What he needed was a US version of the Man With No Name; what he got was a cop named Harry Callahan.

The script of *Dirty Harry*, originally titled *Dead Right*, had passed from Frank Sinatra to Paul Newman, who suggested Eastwood for the role. Malpaso put the package together, with Don Siegel directing.

Filmed in 1971, *Dirty Harry* combined the strongest elements Eastwood had so far demonstrated on screen – the individualism of the Spaghetti Westerns, the

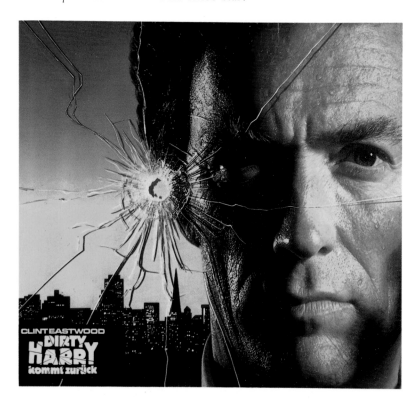

BELOW: Poster artwork for the fourth Dirty Harry *film,* Sudden Impact. *This sequel was hardly sudden and didn't have the impact of its more illustrious predecessor.*

'*When an adult male is chasing an adult female with intent to rape, I shoot the bastard. That's my policy.*'
AS *DIRTY HARRY*

'People in the audience just sit there and say, "I admire the independence. I'd like to have the nerve to tell the boss off or have that control over my life." A lot of people are drawn to an original like Dirty Harry.'
ON *DIRTY HARRY'S* APPEAL

anti-establishment hero of *Coogan's Bluff*, and the laconic humour that was fast becoming his trademark. When the movie opened, in December 1971, Clint knew he had finally found the perfect vehicle. Audiences loved his portrayal of a tough cop, blowing away the bad guys on both sides of the law, leaving a trail of bloody corpses and deflated bureaucrats in his wake. The critical response, however, was far more extreme than the actor had been expecting, with the press viewing Harry's vigilante-like actions as fascistic. Eastwood personally felt the criticism went too far: 'One critic in LA actually wrote that because our killer hijacked a school bus in the movie, we were making an anti-bussing statement. Incredible. Who has time to think of all that crap? We're busy making a movie.' Despite this critical backlash, *Dirty Harry* became a global smash, elevating its central hero to iconic level, much as the Man With No Name had done before, and confirming once and for all Eastwood's position as the king of the box office.

A pattern began to emerge in Eastwood's work in the 1970s, one that would continue throughout his career. Always a savvy businessman, Clint realized that box-office success could give him the room to try other things. So, while building up a more representative canon of work, he continued to experiment with both his screen image and his career behind the camera, often alternating projects to ensure that there was always a sure-fire box-office winner hard on the heels of something more personal.

Joe Kidd (1972) was an exception to this rule. Perhaps Clint's decision to make another Western was in part dictated by the adverse critical reaction to Harry Callahan. The West offered, as always, a world where men were men and their actions weren't judged politically.

Whatever the reasoning, *Joe Kidd*, directed by veteran John Sturges, was a

> 'High Plains Drifter *was great fun because I liked the irony of it, I liked the irony of doing a stylized version of what happens if the sheriff in* High Noon *is killed, and symbolically comes back as some avenging angel or something — and I think that's far more hip than doing just a straight Western.'*

step backwards artistically, something that would become another recurrent trend in Eastwood's work.

High Plains Drifter (1972) was the complete opposite. Where *Joe Kidd* dealt in genre clichés, *High Plains Drifter* was an inventive original with a supernatural tinge and more than a passing nod to Sergio Leone. Opening on the classic image of the lone rider in a barren landscape, *High Plains Drifter* becomes a tale of one town's guilt and the avenging angel who drags them all to hell to pay for it.

Eastwood's character in the movie is clearly playing off the mythology of Leone's gunman, refusing to give his name when asked, biting down on his cigar, and, as always, keeping the dialogue to a bare minimum. The movie was a bold departure for the contemporary Western, proof that Eastwood could expand and redefine the genre that had brought him fame without loosing his sizable audience.

Shortly after Clint had finished filming *High Plains Drifter*, Maggie gave birth, on May 22 1972, to a daughter, Alison, born fifteen days premature.

Eastwood used the box-office success of *High Plains Drifter* to make *Breezy* (1973), the first film he directed without appearing in. 'I've never done a love story,' he reasoned, 'so I'm staying behind the camera.'

Like *Play Misty For Me*, *Breezy* was a low-key production filmed in Carmel, once again focusing on male-female relationships, this time that of an older man (William Holden) and a young hippie girl (Kay Lenz). Eastwood was eager to explore new areas in his work, but what was clear from *Breezy* was that he had absolutely no feeling for this one. It remains a curious period piece, as out of touch with its characters then as it is dated now. Quick to invoke damage control, Eastwood resurrected his box-office

ABOVE: Clint Eastwood displays Magnum Force *(1973).*

'There's nothing wrong with glamorizing the gun. I don't think that hurts anybody. I'm for gun legislation myself. I don't hunt. I love to shoot, but not animals. That turns me off. Besides it's not the bloodletting or whatever people come to see in the movies. It's vengeance. Getting even is a very important thing for the public. They go to work everyday for some guy who's rude and they can't stand and they just have to take it. Then they go see me on the screen and I just kick the shit out of him.'

guarantee character Dirty Harry, in *Magnum Force* (1973). In this movie Harry takes on a covert group of police vigilantes. The debate over Harry's ideology continued in the press – after all, weren't these killer cops doing just what Harry did, only in a more extreme way? – but audiences lapped it up at the box office to the tune of $40 million.

As with the first Harry Callahan adventure, *Magnum Force* was heavily criticized for its violence, an argument its star felt was overblown. 'I feel all this talk about violence in the movies is sort of overdone. You might have, say, ninety people in a movie theatre and one nut and the violence might inspire this one nut to do something and everybody

RIGHT: European front-of-house still for Thunderbolt and Lightfoooot *(1974).*

CLINT EASTWOOD
dans
LE CANARDEUR
(THUNDERBOLT AND LIGHTFOOT)

LE CANARDEUR

avec
JEFF BRIDGES
et
GEORGE KENNEDY
dans le rôle de "LEARY"
United Artists

blames it on the movies. But we can't worry about that one nut.'

Thunderbolt and Lightfoot (1974) kept Eastwood in the present tense, but this time he was on the other side of the law. Like *Breezy* it was a movie that explored the relationship between the young and the old, in this case ageing robber Eastwood — looking to pull that last big score — and young drifter Jeff Bridges. At the height of his box-office powers, Eastwood took a risk by casting himself as the older partner; he also took a chance on rookie director Michael Cimino, who four years later directed the Oscar-winning *The Deer Hunter* (1978).

Eastwood took the directing seat once again for the mountain-climbing thriller *The Eiger Sanction* (1975), but only out of necessity. 'I couldn't find another director willing to climb up and down mountains and dangle several thousand feet above the valley floor.' As visually impressive as the movie was, Eastwood, who trained for months beforehand, lost heart in the project when one of the production's climbers, Dave Knowles, was tragically killed by falling rocks while filming on the Eiger.

LEFT: If a job's worth doing... Eastwood scales the heights of The Eiger Sanction *(1975).*

LOVE AND A MONKEY

'I first saw the "star" thing in my son. He'd see people coming up to me, paying attention or asking for autographs and he'd ask me, "How come people ask you to sign papers?" I said: "Well, they see me in the theatres and it's sort of a custom that some jerk invented years ago."'

ON HANDLING FAME

FACING PAGE: Breathing new life into the Western – The Outlaw Josey Wales *(1976).*

Now firmly established as the number-one box-office star in the United States, Eastwood was maintaining a low-key private life. The small-town atmosphere of Carmel afforded him some anonymity and, when that wasn't enough, he would occasionally don hat and dark glasses so he and Maggie could go to the local cinema unnoticed. His first daughter Kimber was still a well kept secret, although he visited Roxanne and the child about four times a year.

'What I do, I do the best. Maybe I'm not as versatile as other actors, but for the type of thing I do, I do it well.'

This peaceful, organized private life was about to change.

Sondra Locke was a young, petite blonde actress who had previously auditioned unsuccessfully for the lead in *Breezy*. Her career had begun in style, with an Oscar nomination for her role in *The Heart is a Lonely Hunter* (1968). Subsequent work had failed to live up to this promise, however. In 1975 she was living in Hollywood with Gordon Anderson. Theirs was an unusual relationship – Anderson was her best friend and, years before, the couple had married, although most people who knew them believed it was a marriage in name only.

Having played around in the action-adventure field, Eastwood had decided the time was right for another Western. The genre was on the decline in Hollywood, and in many ways he might have looked on *The Outlaw Josey Wales* (1976) as a fitting epitaph. Sondra Locke auditioned and was cast for the lead role opposite Eastwood. Based on the book *Gone To Texas* by Cherokee oral historian Forrest Carter, *The Outlaw Josey Wales* had all the hallmarks of a classic Western, with Eastwood as the rancher forced to seek revenge after the massacre of his family. Philip Kaufman was commissioned to write the screenplay and to direct, but after the first week of shooting Eastwood fired him and took over directing the picture himself.

While away on location, Eastwood and Locke began an affair. In his life as a 'married bachelor' this was not a new occurrence for Clint, but his relationship with Locke was different, something that would be reflected in their partnership on screen and result in the end of the actor's marriage.

When *Josey Wales* was released, it was hailed as one of the best Westerns of the decade, with the critics agreeing Eastwood the director had delivered his most accomplished film to date.

Having finally made some headway with the critics, Eastwood perversely chose to alienate them once again by dragging Harry Callahan out of moth-balls. *The Enforcer* (1976) was billed as 'the Dirtyest Harry of them all'. Tyne Daly was drafted in to act as feminist foil to reactionary Callahan, while the vio-lence quota was kept high, producing a film clearly designed to give the fans what they wanted . . . and very little else. Its US gross of $24 million proved that the movie was bang on target.

Since its inception, Malpaso had been housed on the Universal lot but, now that Universal had begun its studio tour, Eastwood found his privacy invaded. 'I'd walk out of my office and the bus would be there with people yelling.' Consequently, he moved Malpaso to Warner Bros, where he rapidly became that company's most valuable asset.

Off screen, Eastwood's relationship with Sondra Locke was progressing; and he bought her a mansion in Bel Air. On screen, things were also going well between the couple. *The Gauntlet* (1977) had been mooted as a possible vehicle for Eastwood and Barbra Streisand; instead he cast Locke in what was to be the most expensive Malpaso production to date. For all its high action and excessive set pieces – including firing eight thousand rounds of ammo at a shack that then col-lapses – the movie was allowing Eastwood to experiment further with his

ABOVE: Enforcing the law – Harry Callahan is back!

image by playing, for once, an inept detective. This subtle deconstruction of the macho persona he had spent his career building up was a theme he would continue throughout his 1980s work and beyond.

As successful as Clint was in the late 1970s, there was still one large strand of the market he hadn't tapped into – the kids. *Every Which Way but Loose* (1978) was a conscious attempt to do just that, teaming the actor with an orang-utan named Clyde in a low-brow comedy that became the star's biggest box-office success to date. In North America alone, *Every Which Way but Loose* took $48 million, making it the second highest grossing movie of 1978 after *Superman*; Eastwood's deal with Warners meant he saw an amazing 42 percent of the gross. As if confirmation were needed, his box-office dominance was highlighted when he appeared with Burt Reynolds on the cover of *Time* under the headline 'Good ole Burt, Cool-Eyed Clint'.

Taking time off from his new-found hobby of racing his $150,000 Ferrari, Eastwood re-teamed with Don Siegel for his next project, *Escape from Alcatraz* (1979). The true story of prisoner Frank Morris, the only man believed ever to have escaped from the prison, was their least happy collaboration. Eastwood controlled the money while Siegel owned the script, and both had their own ideas of how the movie should go.

Maggie Eastwood legally separated from her husband in February 1979 after 26 years of marriage. 'I've misbehaved. But I have always tried to make it up,' he said. Eastwood's extramarital relationships had always been discreetly handled, but his affair with Sondra Locke was public knowledge and that proved too much for Maggie.

Eastwood's final career decision of the 1970s turned out to be a wise one.

LEFT: Eastwood checks in — Escape from Alcatraz *(1979).*

Francis Ford Coppola offered him the lead in *Apocalypse Now*. 'I know Conrad's *Heart of Darkness*, I read it in school, but I still don't understand the ending of your script,' he told the director. Eastwood was used to relatively short shooting periods; when Coppola was still on location in the jungle 18 months later, he knew he'd made the right choice.

A NEW DECADE,
A NEW APPROACH

'There are few careers in Hollywood as solid
as Clint's. He's gone beyond being an actor.
He's one of the most respected directors we
have, with his own production company, and,
in short, he's a filmmaker concerned with
maintaining an image of strength, as did Gary
Cooper and John Wayne, with whom he has
every right to be bracketed.'
WILLIAM HOLDEN

FACING PAGE: Bronco Billy *ushers in the 1980s.*

*RIGHT: Sondra Locke —
the knives are out?*
Bronco Billy *(1980).*

The 1980s proved an eventful decade for Clint Eastwood. On the positive side, he continued to develop his talents and range by placing increasing emphasis on the more personal movies he alternated with his overtly commercial projects. On the negative side, his private life exploded in the media, and

> *'Here was a guy who was a loser but who wouldn't acknowledge it, and who was a hold-out against cynicism. It wasn't old-fashioned but in a way it was. The guy was fun to play because he had to be stripped of all his dignity.'*
> ON BRONCO BILLY

by the close of the decade, his grip on the box office had seriously diminished.

Nevertheless, the decade began well. The National Association of Theatre Owners presented him with a distinguished career award in February 1980. *Breezy* star William Holden did the honours at the ceremony.

'He's more open and vocal, and, being expressive of his feelings, he's vulnerable. He believes in God and country, and goes around preaching old-fashioned ethics to kids like, "Say your prayers before you go to bed." And yet, he's an ex-convict. He's also like a messiah to this little ragtag band of losers. It's almost a statement of loyalty in the way he keeps them from giving up.'
ON BRONCO BILLY

Eastwood quickly set the agenda for this stage of his career with *Bronco Billy* (1980), playing the washed-up proprietor of a struggling Wild West show whose players included Sondra Locke.

This expansion of Eastwood's traditional image won favour once again with the critics, and the movie is now considered a watershed moment in his career. It was an effective note on which to usher in his decade of greatest change. Effectively shot even by Eastwood's stan-

dards, *Bronco Billy* came in 13 days ahead of schedule and $830,000 under budget.

An astute businessman right from the start of his career, Eastwood had amassed a personal fortune that many rumoured made him the wealthiest actor alive. Determined to keep hold of as much of it as he could in the impending divorce from Maggie, he formed a new company, Robert Daley Productions, to protect profits from all future productions.

Despite the critical rewards of *Bronco Billy*, the film's lacklustre performance at the box office prompted Eastwood to reply with a keep-'em-happy sequel to *Every Which Way but Loose*, offering the director's chair to long-time stuntman Buddy Van Horn. 'I was at home and I got a phone call,' Van Horn recalled. 'It was Clint saying, "I've got this script here. Why don't you check it out, and if you like it, you can direct it." My jaw dropped. I told him, "I already like it."'

The film, *Any Which Way You Can* (1980), reunited Eastwood with orangutan Clyde, provided another co-starring role for Locke, saw Eastwood duet on the soundtrack with Ray Charles, made a rapid $40 million at the box office and was without doubt the actor's lamest film since *Ambush at Cimarron Pass*.

Nonetheless, Eastwood clearly enjoyed the fact that he had tapped into a younger market, and he was determined to explore it further. In 1977 *Star Wars* had changed forever the shape of cinema. Special-effects movies meant big box office, and Eastwood thought it was time he gave one a go.

The result was *Firefox* (1982), based on the 1977 novel by Craig Thomas, which blended Cold War ideology with aerial pyrotechnics and was clearly a misjudged dud. The young audience Eastwood had tried to mine were into robots, Wookies and galaxies far, far away, not some middle-aged man keeping the Communists at bay with what were, by the state of the art, some pretty ropy effects.

Certainly the movie was a costly mistake for Eastwood. Convinced it was the right move, he had gambled a budget of $18 million, the largest for any of his movies to date. At a time when financial matters were already on his mind, Eastwood was particularly aware of this loss, because *Firefox* marked his debut as producer as well as director.

With typical frugality, *Honkytonk Man* (1982), the movie that followed, was one of Eastwood's small-scale, more personal

LEFT: Eastwood dons fly-boy uniform in the lamentable Firefox *(1982).*

Honkytonk Man

LEFT: Singing, strumming and dying – Honkytonk Man (1982).

films, and made it clear that this was now the pattern he wished his work to maintain. 'It's not a formal arrangement with the studio. I know they find shoot-'em-ups appealing and they know I like to strike out, not always do the same thing.'

Honkytonk Man, set in the Depression era of his childhood, was by no means the same thing. Eastwood played Red Stovall, a failed country and western singer, dying of tuberculosis, making one final journey to Nashville in the hope of playing at the famed Grand Ole Opry.

Along for the journey is his nephew Whit, played by Eastwood's son Kyle. As he had done with *Firefox*, Clint produced as well as directed; in addition, as the role demanded, he sang and accompanied himself on guitar.

In the 1970s, Dirty Harry had stood as an iconoclast; in the more conservative Reagan-era 1980s he re-emerged as an

---

'When you get to the end, you don't want to have 'em say, "Well, he did fifteen cop dramas and twenty Westerns and that was it." It's nice to have those others too.'
ON HONKYTONK MAN

---

icon with *Sudden Impact* (1983). Mindful that three of his last four movies had failed to deliver at the box office, Eastwood turned once again to that sure thing, Harry Callahan. However, *Sudden Impact*, this time produced and directed by its star, became more than just another sequel. The change in US politics

brought Harry into a new light. Ronald Reagan's old-fashioned gung-ho attitude saw Harry, once labelled a fascist, now declared a hero. The impact was most strongly felt when the President himself adopted Callahan's latest catchphrase, 'Go ahead, make my day!' In typical Eastwood fashion, the character had remained constant . . . but all those around him had changed.

Released at Christmas 1983, *Sudden Impact* became the most financially successful Harry Callahan movie yet, with Eastwood himself picking up a reported $30 million, something to tide him over in light of his impending divorce.

As his follow-up, Eastwood chose *Tightrope* (1984). Screenwriter Richard Tuggle (who had scripted *Escape From Alcatraz*) sent Eastwood the script with himself attached as director. Much to his surprise, Eastwood accepted the project. In the character of Wes Block, a cop with a far darker psyche than that of Harry Callahan, the actor recognized an opportunity to cross the two strands of his career. *Tightrope* was firmly in the populist cop vein, but the self-doubting role of Block offered him a chance to expand that image of the cop, blurring the line between hero and villain.

FACING PAGE: 'Go ahead, make my day' – Dirty Harry finds political favour in Sudden Impact *(1983).*

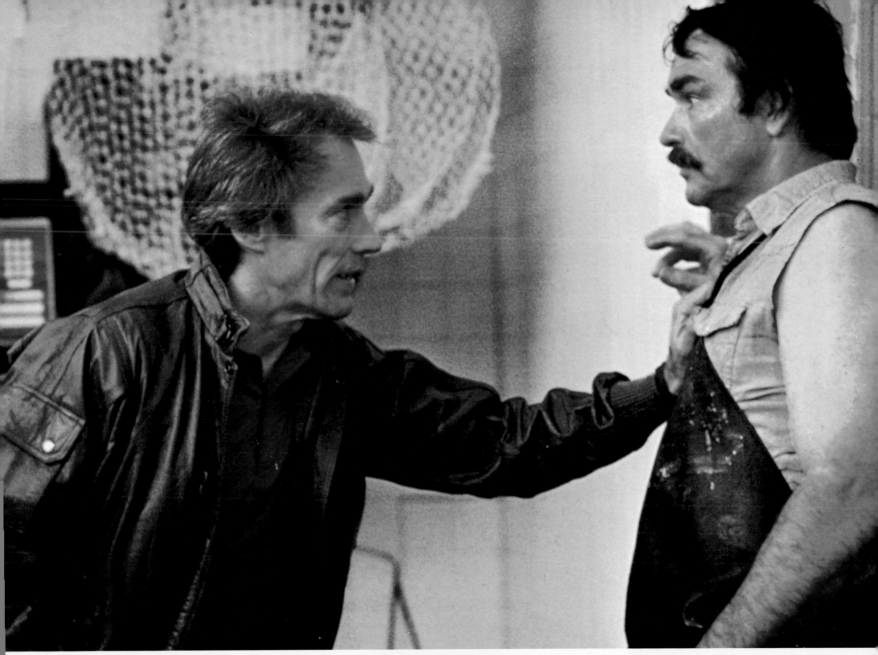

SUDDEN IMPACT

830169

Feeling that Kyle had had a fair shot at acting, Eastwood offered the same opportunity to his daughter Alison, who played Block's daughter and the subject of an attempted rape by the killer; this would shortly after be echoed in real life, when Alison Eastwood was herself stalked by obsessed fan Mike Joynson. As with *Honkytonk Man*, *Tightrope* let the critics know there was a new Clint Eastwood in town; unlike *Honkytonk Man*, however, it proved that audiences were eager to see Eastwood explore these new avenues on film.

Why he chose to follow it with a movie as witless as *City Heat* (1984) is anyone's guess. True, it looked like a sure thing on paper – throughout the 1980s Eastwood and Burt Reynolds were the two biggest stars in the United States; casting them in a movie together surely couldn't fail. Yet this Prohibition-era gangster comedy did, on every level.

'If I just wanted to go out and make some dough I could gun 'em down as good as I ever did. But I'd rather not do movies where there are 800 guys in the theatre and one chick who was coerced into going by her brother.'

The damage was luckily minimal. Eastwood's new direction in his work was rewarded with a retrospective at the Museum of Modern Art in New York. This was followed by a similar season at the Cinématheque in Paris, where Eastwood was awarded the Chevalier des Arts et Lettres by the French Ministry of Culture; retrospectives at the Filmmuseum in Munich and in London followed.

Eastwood was undoubtedly pleased finally to be receiving recognition without having changed to suit his detractors.

In 1985 Eastwood was finally divorced by Maggie after a six-year separation. He stipulated that the divorce settlement remain undisclosed. Alarms should have been sounding for Sondra Locke, too, when actress Carrie Snodgress took what could easily have been her role in her partner's next movie, *Pale Rider* (1985).

As he had with *The Outlaw Josey Wales*, Eastwood felt the time was right for a Western. He was right. Filmed on location in Sun Valley, Idaho, *Pale Rider* owed more than a passing debt to *High Plains Drifter* but, unusually for Eastwood, he originated the script from scratch, beginning once again with the classic idea of the lone stranger riding into town.

The following May, Eastwood hired a yacht to launch the film in official competition in Cannes, where it was critically praised before its opening in the United States in June. It took over $21 million in its first ten days, proving that once again the combination of Clint Eastwood and the Western was unbeatable.

HIS HONOUR, THE MAYOR

'I stood for office because, at a time in my life when I was no longer totally satisfied with my celebrity, I was tempted to go in a new direction. When you know that you already have the audience waiting for you, the temptation is very great.'
AS MAYOR OF CARMEL, 1986

FACING PAGE: Taking some time off, the Mayor of Carmel in Heartbreak Ridge *(1986).*

Although Sondra Locke's working relationship with Clint Eastwood was never exclusive, Hollywood perceived it as such, and offers to her of work in non-Malpaso productions were all but nonexistent. Offers from Eastwood were likewise few on the ground, so she decided to take a stab at directing. For her debut movie, *Ratboy*

'I said that he had used my "Go ahead, make my day!" line from Sudden Impact, *so I had borrowed his "Get government off our backs" line. He said he was envious of the vote margin.'*

MAYOR EASTWOOD ON HIS CONVERSATION WITH PRESIDENT REAGAN

(1986), she used Eastwood's regular crew. They were free because their boss had other things on his mind in early 1986 – local politics.

Eastwood's desire to run for Mayor of Carmel dated back to 1983, when he had battled with the local planning commis-sion over building on land he owned opposite his Hog's Breath Inn. 'I started thinking, "If this can happen to me, who has visibility and access to the press, imagine what happens to the little guy who is trying to get a project through. Imagine if that project was my whole life, my whole life's savings and family's future were riding on it." It doesn't take too much imagination for me to put myself in that position. You're dealing with people's lives and they deserve respect.'

He announced himself as a candidate on January 30 1986, instantly guarantee-ing this local election world-wide cover-age. 'I've lived here a lot of years,' he said. 'I want to give something back to the community.'

On April 8 he won by a landslide, garnering 2166 votes, about 72 percent of the voters. Ronald Reagan was among those who phoned to congratulate him.

His mother Ruth and sister Jean attended the swearing-in ceremony the following week. The job ran two years and paid a token $50 a week. Eastwood wasted no time in getting going. Within four weeks, four of the planning commis-sioners who had originally stalled his redevelopment work were replaced.

Numerous achievements came during his time as mayor. Chain stores were allowed into ultra-conservative Carmel for the first time. Most notably, he gave permission for a take-out ice-cream shop called Chocolate Dreams to open, which had previously – and very publicly – been denied. (During the campaign the opposition had put out posters aping the *Josey Wales* poster art, with Josey brandishing ice-cream cones as opposed to guns: 'Law, order and ice cream,' ran the slogan.)

During his two-year stint as mayor, Eastwood also found time to make three more movies, the first of which was the tough talkin' drama *Heartbreak Ridge* (1986). Based on the Marines' invasion of

LEFT: Taking on the town planners? Heartbreak Ridge *(1986).*

ABOVE: *Fulfilling a life-long dream – Clint Eastwood brings the life and music of Charlie Parker to the big screen in* Bird *(1988).*

Grenada, *Heartbreak Ridge* began filming with the full backing of the US Defense Department – although they withdrew their support when they viewed the final cut. The movie certainly delivered on the action front but, with grizzled Gunnery Sergeant Tom Highway, Eastwood once again had a role that allowed him to re-examine and dissect the macho image that had made his name.

The second film Eastwood made in this period was to be his most personal project to date. *Bird* (1988) was the biopic of jazz great Charlie Parker, and marked only the third time the actor had directed without starring. (In addition to *Breezy*, Eastwood had directed Sondra Locke and Harvey Keitel in 'Vanessa in the Garden', a 1985 episode of Steven Spielberg's TV series *Amazing Stories*.) *Bird* was very much a labour of love and, while he knew it was unlikely to turn much of a profit, Eastwood felt, having pursued the script for eight years, he had given enough back to Warners to be allowed this indulgence.

While the movie was in pre-production, Eastwood met Parker's widow, Chan Richardson, in Paris, and she provided him with several tapes of Parker's performances that had been long presumed lost. Musical supervisor Lennie Niehaus digitally remixed these for the movie's soundtrack, and later picked up an Oscar for Best Achievement in Sound.

Niehaus was not the only one getting awards for the acclaimed *Bird*. Forest Whitaker, who played the title role, received the Best Actor at the Cannes Film Festival, while Eastwood took home a Golden Globe for Best Director.

In 1988 Eastwood retired as Mayor of Carmel, quashing rumours that he would

LEFT: Directing the award-winning Forest Whitaker in Bird *(1988).*

continue in political office, perhaps one day even run for President.

Eastwood appreciated the risk Warners took with him on *Bird*, so for his next movie he revived the cash cow that was Dirty Harry.

The Dead Pool (1988) was filmed during the final days of Eastwood's time as mayor. Despite an appearance by comic-superstar-in-the-making Jim Carrey, it was by far the weakest of the Harry Callahan movies, due in part to Buddy Van Horn's leaden direction but more so to Eastwood's going-through-the-motions performance. The humour quota was upped, so audiences were given the

'If I am convincing as Harry it is because I am a good actor. Harry is a bitter man, a bastard who fights against laws that he considers too inflexible, and I believe that's a role I play well. On the screen, that is, not in real life.'

uneasy impression that, throughout the movie, the actor was quietly sending up his most popular alter ego.

The Dead Pool was clearly a disappointment to Dirty Harry fans and Eastwood supporters alike. More than anything, for the first time the actor had started to lookhis age. A whole slew of younger

'It's humorous, lots of "make my day"-type lines, very good action sequences. Sure I've played this before.'
ON THE ROOKIE

leading men — Tom Cruise, Kevin Costner and Tom Hanks among them — were coming into their own in the late 1980s and early 1990s, and alongside them Eastwood was beginning to seem anachronistic and jaded. It was clearly a problem that worried him, leading him in the course of the next three years to make two of his best — and two of his worst — movies.

Pink Cadillac (1989) definitely ranks in the 'worst' category. A comedy road movie co-starring Bernadette Peters, it is distinguished by two facts: first, it remains the only Eastwood movie since the 1950s never to have been granted a theatrical release in the UK (it went straight to video); second, while filming, Clint met an actress named Frances Fisher.

Eastwood soon became closely involved with Fisher, despite the presence of Locke in his life. In April 1989, while Locke was directing her second film, *Impulse* (1990), she received a letter addressed to Mrs Gordon Anderson (throughout her relationship with Clint, she had remained married). It informed her that the locks on their Bel Air home had been changed and her possessions placed in storage. 'I told him I couldn't

believe that was all he had to say to me after 13 years,' Locke remembered.

For the first time in his career, Eastwood's very private life was made public when Locke retaliated by suing for palimony, with allegations of two abortions and a sterilization operation performed, she claimed, at Eastwood's insistence. She also asked the court to ban the actor from their house: 'I know him to have a terrible temper and he has frequently been abusive to me.' The couple settled out of court in March 1991, with one of the stipulations of the agreement being that she would never divulge details of their private life to the media.

Eastwood's tabloid profile was kept high during this year when the child he had been hiding for 25 years finally became public knowledge. Eastwood's relationship with Kimber – who had named her son Clinton – is said to have cooled off after she revealed the identity of her father to the press.

Eastwood reacted to all this adversity by heading off to Africa to make one of his best movies. Despite having flopped with *Pink Cadillac*, his eye was temporarily off the box office when he decided to make *White Hunter, Black Heart* (1990). Published in 1953, Peter Viertel's novel of the same title was a fictionalized account of the making of the movie *The African Queen* (1951). Eastwood's character was closely modelled on director John Huston, and in researching the role he consulted with Huston's daughter, the actress Anjelica Huston. He also read Huston's autobiography and watched his television interviews.

Once again Eastwood debuted the movie at Cannes. *White Hunter, Black Heart* delighted critics, particularly in Europe, where Eastwood has always been more appreciated. Its critical success in many ways paved the way for *Unforgiven*, which would come two years later.

The Rookie (1990), however, showed that it was not Eastwood's intention to concentrate solely on quality movies. Co-starring Charlie Sheen, it was a blatant attempt to revitalize his flagging box-office appeal.

On every level *The Rookie* was a disaster, leaving little more than the impression that Clint Eastwood, once the biggest star in the world, just didn't know how to deliver the goods any more.

FACING PAGE: A woman and a car – Eastwood with Bernadette Peters and a Pink Cadillac *(1989).*

BACK IN THE SADDLE

'I'm not sure this will be my last Western but, if it is, it'll be the perfect one. The fellow I play is living on the edge of Hell most of the time. He's really a tormented person.'
ON UNFORGIVEN

FACING PAGE: Clint Eastwood with Meryl Streep in the acclaimed Bridges of Madison County *(1995).*

David Webb Peoples wrote *The William Munny Killings* in the mid-1970s. Eastwood had bought the screenplay, and had been holding on to it until he was old enough to play the lead role.

Eastwood had avoided the Western since 1985's *Pale Rider*. *Unforgiven* (1992) mined the same vein he had been working, demythologizing the West. The character of William Munny was that of a gunslinger who didn't die young, just slowly faded away. In a traditional Western his riding off to avenge an abused prostitute should have been a heroic deed, a moment of much-needed revitalization, a rebirth for the hero; in *Unforgiven* Eastwood turned it into a dark, sombre meditation of the soul, a man forced to confront his past and his own being by once again picking up a gun. The characters of *Unforgiven* should have been shot down in their prime: now they were coming to grips with still being alive.

Eastwood knew he had a winner in *Unforgiven*, and for once he decided to surround himself with an all-star cast, including Gene Hackman, Morgan Freeman and Richard Harris. Frances Fisher, who would make Eastwood a father for the fourth time with the birth of Francesca Ruth in 1992, was cast as Strawberry Alice, the madam of the whorehouse.

The production shot for 55 days in Alberta, Canada, with Eastwood persuading the cast and crew to work for 21 hours straight on the final day in order to avoid a snowfall that would have delayed the completion and pushed the movie beyond its $14.4 million budget (a relatively minuscule amount for a studio movie in 1992, let alone one with this kind of cast). The end credits carry a dedication to both Sergio Leone and Don Siegel, Eastwood the director acknowl-

BELOW: William Munny rides again – Unforgiven (1992).

edging his two greatest influences, both of whom had recently died.

The groundswell of critical support that had been building for Clint Eastwood as a moviemaker erupted with the release of *Unforgiven*. But what surprised everyone, including its star, was how much the audience support echoed that of the critics. *Unforgiven* opened in late summer 1992 to the highest-ever

> *He was very explicit about his desire to demythologize violence. I'm really glad Clint convinced me this was not a Clint Eastwood film!'*
> GENE HACKMAN

box-office returns for an August weekend. And the success continued, rapidly pushing the movie past the $100 million mark in the United States alone.

Unforgiven's commercial success was soon duplicated when the awards season came round. It picked up Best Picture and Best Director Golden Globes, the National Film Critics award for Best Picture, Director and Actor, and the

Director's Guild Award for Best Director of the year. Eastwood's greatest success ever was capped off with a total of nine Oscar nominations announced in February 1993.

On March 29 1993 Clint Eastwood, who had last attended the Oscar ceremony back in 1973, received Academy Awards for Best Director and Best Film. In addition, Gene Hackman won his second Oscar, for Best Supporting Actor. Eastwood thanked his

LEFT: Eastwood on the Oscar trail.

> *'I didn't make it with any commercial results in mind. If I had I'd probably have changed certain things, but I tried not to compromise on it.'*
> ON UNFORGIVEN

mother Ruth, who was in attendance, in his acceptance speech.

Just a year before, Eastwood's career had looked as it were coming to the end of the line. *Unforgiven* completely turned things around, as he finally earned the respect as a moviemaker he had always desired and so richly deserved. *In the Line of Fire* (1993) the following summer proved the actor was back on top to stay. Portraying a gripping cat-and-mouse game between a secret service man (Eastwood) and a presidential assassin (John Malkovich), it was another $100-million hit.

Following these two successes, Eastwood donned his directing hat and reassembled the Malpaso team once more for *A Perfect World* (1993), a darkly brooding character piece that cast Kevin Costner against type as an escaped con-

vict being tracked down by Eastwood's lawman. The movie was a modest success, but not the blockbuster that had been expected from the casting of two such big-name stars. What was clear from *A Perfect World*, however, was how much Eastwood was enjoying sharing the screen with other actors of equal stature. Having played the loner for so long, he clearly relished the opportunity to work opposite the likes of Gene Hackman, Morgan Freeman and Costner. His next movie would follow this trend.

The Bridges of Madison County (published in 1992) was a slim romantic novel that had unexpectedly taken the United States by storm, selling over 9 million copies. The movie rights to Robert James Waller's book were quickly snapped up by Hollywood, passing from the likes of Steven Spielberg and Sydney Pollack, eventually landing with Eastwood.

He cast himself as photographer Robert Kincaid; Meryl Streep won the role of Francesca, the Italian housewife living in Iowa. Watching Eastwood in *The Bridges of Madison County* (1995) gives a perfect opportunity to study his acting technique: while Streep is rather mannered and active, Eastwood remains still, composed and totally in command.

Adding a rare romantic side to his character on screen, this was rightly praised as one of his finest performances.

In the five decades Clint Eastwood has been working in cinema he has created a career unparalleled in Hollywood history. The figurehead of a major movement in the Western genre, he provided the essential link between Europe's reinterpretation and the history of the West. He brought these ideas back home and continued to explore the mythology of the Western, creating or helping to create the finest examples of the genre to have emerged in the last three decades. He adapted the Western hero and ideology to the modern day, generating one of cinema's greatest icons along the way. Off-screen, Eastwood's work has been equally ground-breaking: he took control of his career at a time when the studios dominated everything and everyone, and so he constructed a template that every successful actor since has emulated. With an almost unerring ability to satisfy his audience, Eastwood has always striven to enlarge it, succeeding on many occasions with movies as diverse as *Unforgiven*, *Bird* and *Bronco Billy*. In between, he has established himself as one of the modern US cinema's best directors.

In 1996, Eastwood becomes eligible for his pension; thankfully he shows no sign of slowing down. He returns to the action field yet again in the thriller *Absolute Power* (1996) and has recently, and unexpectedly, married a 26-year-old.

Eastwood once said, 'I guess I revere the individual, which is why I've been attracted to playing individualist kind of characters on screen.' He remains Hollywood's truest individual.

ABOVE: Portrait of the awarding-winning photographer, Eastwood as Robert Kincaid in Bridges of Madison County *(1995).*